# Affiliate Marketing for Beginners

*Learn How to Build Your Own Affiliate Marketing Business and Start Making Passive Income Today*

By

## Robert J. Murphy

# Table of Contents

# Introduction

I want to thank you and congratulate you for downloading the book, "Affiliate Marketing: Affiliate Marketing Beginners Guide to Build Your Own Affiliate Marketing Business and Start Making Passive Income from Home Now."

It is everybody's dream to earn a passive income or make money while sleeping. What if I told you that this was easier than you thought and there are many ways in which you can earn money without actively taking part in the process? Would you take the opportunity?

Well, I'm telling you that there is a way that you can make a passive income. Yes, that's correct. It is easy to earn a passive income by engaging in affiliate marketing. Affiliation is the process of tying up with merchants and promoting their products for a return fee.

If you happen to be popular on the Internet and wish to capitalize on it, then you happen to be just the right candidate for affiliate marketing. This book has been written with the intention of helping you understand the process involved with affiliate marketing and how you can get started on it.

Thanks again for downloading this book. I hope you enjoy it!

# Chapter One:

# What is Affiliate Marketing?

Affiliate marketing is a passive income opportunity where merchants create products and use third-party resources for marketing purposes. Essentially, the third party is responsible for marketing the product to their audience. In the process, the third party earns a profit known as passive income. There are four unique parties involved in affiliate marketing: merchants, affiliates, customers, and networks.

## Merchant

Merchants are the creators of the products or the brand. They are the retailers or sellers that are selling the product which affiliate marketers are marketing. Merchants are responsible for product creation, as well as for discovering affiliates that they wish to work with. Any company with products to sell can fall under the "merchant" category when it comes to affiliate marketing. This means that a merchant may be a large corporation such as Microsoft, Dyson, or Philips. Or, it may be a sole proprietor of a company who is looking to increase their sales volumes. As long as the seller has something to sell, they can be considered merchants.

## Affiliates

Affiliates are the ones responsible for marketing the products as per their agreement with the merchant. Affiliates may be called "publishers" by some, as they are publishing marketing content on behalf of the merchant. An affiliate may be an individual or it may be a company, but either way it is someone who has agreed with the merchant to promote products and services to its audience. In affiliate agreements, the primary element is that the affiliate will promote products on behalf of the merchant, and as a result, they earn a profit. The profit is typically a percentage of all sales made through their unique affiliate link or with their unique affiliate code. For those who get involved and are effective at marketing, this business can be extremely lucrative. People make anywhere from hundreds to thousands of dollars each month through this process. It is an extremely simple income-building strategy that essentially only requires you to post a few links to your business page or social media pages and encourage your existing audience to shop with the merchant. When they do, you are paid.

## Customers

Customers are a critical element of the affiliate marketing program. They are the reason the system is kept alive, since they are the ones who are making the purchases. In other words, customers are the reason that affiliate marketers can even earn a profit using this model. Each time a customer clicks the link provided on your affiliate posts, they are directed to the merchant's website, where they can purchase products or services. When they do, you earn profit as a result.

The best part about customers in this program is that they are often eager to click the links. In many cases, merchants offer unique discounts to those purchasing through affiliate links. As a result, the customers are more likely to go look for affiliate links and purchase through them so they can gain the discount. As long as it is your link they purchase through, you are guaranteed to earn a profit. So all you have to do is make your link findable.

Social networks are one of the easiest places to access customers. When you build an audience through social networking, you develop a system of people who trust you and look to you for advice and inspiration. Some may follow you loyally, and others may recognize you by seeing you on their page frequently. As a result of this familiarity, they develop a trust in you which makes them more likely to purchase the items that you recommend. In addition to this being easier for an affiliate marketer to market on these platforms, this also happens to be where most customers go to look for the codes in the first place. While many customers know that they are purchasing from third-party affiliate links and do so intentionally, many others will simply click through because they are interested in the product and will have no idea that they've even contributed to you earning an income.

The best part about the entire program for customers is that they do not have to pay extra for products in order for you to get paid. They will pay the same amount or, in many cases, they may even get a special discount for purchasing through you. The affiliation of the entire process runs in the background without otherwise interfering with the customer's purchasing process. This means that if they didn't know that they were using an affiliate link, they would never find out. The entire affiliation program runs in the background as a part of the sale, and not as any special agreement or term that the customer enters into. The affiliation deal is strictly between the affiliate and the merchant.

## Network

The network is essentially the connection between affiliates and merchants. While most aren't even aware of the fact that they are a part of a network, they are. In some cases, the network is smaller. It may be a link on a merchant's page, and when the soon-to-be affiliate clicks it, they become a part of the merchant's unique network.

In other circumstances, both the affiliate and the merchant may intentionally join a networking site, such as Clickbank or ShareASale, to make their connection. Here, affiliates are offered the opportunity to apply for affiliate programs with many different companies and are awarded their programs through the networking site. In many cases, the programs are awarded based on the affiliate's audience, including who is in the audience and typically the size of the audience also. Don't let this fool you, though. You do not need a massive audience to begin with affiliate marketing.

Some affiliates go through with the affiliate marketing programs that they are connected with as an opportunity to make a sale while they promote products. For example, having their name connected with a high-end product through an affiliate program is a great way to increase their perceived worth on social media, thus increasing their online popularity. Others, however, go through with these programs as an opportunity to try new products and share their results with their audience. There are many reasons why you may be interested in getting into affiliate marketing yourself, but either way, it is a great opportunity to earn a profit and, in some cases, earn free products as well.

# Chapter Two:

## FAQs

As you learn more about affiliate marketing, you are definitely going to have some questions come up. This concept is entirely new for some people, so naturally you want to make sure that you are clear on what the concept is and how it works. To help you out, here are some common questions that people ask about affiliate marketing.

## Is affiliate marketing legal?

Yes, affiliate marketing is legal. You will only be providing a link to a product rather than mentioning the product directly on your website or blog. It is up to your customers to decide whether or not they wish to click on the link without you forcing them. Essentially, you are suggesting a product and people are making the personal decision to purchase or not.

## Are affiliate marketing and AdSense the same?

No. AdSense is a type of affiliate marketing that is run by Google. You can sign up with AdSense and AdWords if you wish to make the most of your affiliation. You can have both affiliate marketing and AdSense running on your blog.

## How do I start with affiliate marketing?

Affiliate marketing is a simple concept to adopt if you go about it the right way. You have to find companies that have affiliation programs running so that you can tie up with them and start promoting their products. You can do a simple Google search to find such companies and sign up for them. But make sure you find the right programs and companies to ensure that you are not tying up with companies that are spurious. In this book, we will look at some companies that are popular for their affiliate programs.

## How do I choose the right products to promote?

For this, you have first to identify the niche market and start your website or blog. Based on it, companies will approach you, or you can approach companies to promote products. For example, if you are in the fitness industry, then you can promote supplements, weight loss equipment, etc. We will read about this in detail in the next chapter.

## Is it essential to have a blog or website for affiliate marketing?

In short, no. You can definitely engage in affiliate marketing without a blog or website, although it will be much easier to get started if you do have one. Alternatives to having a blog or website, however, include paid per click advertising and other advertising forms to promote products, and social media. In fact, many affiliate marketers work solely through social media and don't have any form of personal website at all. Recently, Instagram and YouTube have really grown in terms of how they can help affiliate marketers increase their promoting abilities and earn a greater profit.

## Is affiliation chargeable?

No. Affiliate marketing is free of cost. There are no charges involved while signing up. But there will be some costs involved in the promotion process and the method you choose. If you choose to blog, then it will not cost you, but if you choose PPC, then you might have to incur some costs, such as email marketing, advertising, etc. If you come across any program that is asking you to pay upfront, then it might be a fraud site.

## Do I need any specific degrees to be an affiliate?

No. Your educational background hardly matters, and it is only your online popularity that counts. If you have excellent marketing skills, then it will help you and earn you more significant revenue.

## How much can I earn through affiliates?

The sky is the limit. You can make anywhere from $100 to $5000 through affiliate marketing. You have to make the most of the popularity that you have and tie up with well-paying affiliates to earn more each week. Once you get going, you will see that your income is consistently growing.

## How often will I get paid?

The payment schedule will be based on which particular company you choose to go with. Some pay out on a weekly basis, others bi-weekly, some are monthly, and some pay out when you hit a certain threshold. Furthermore, some will accrue your money in an affiliate account and you can choose to cash out once you hit a certain earning value.

In order to know when you are going to get paid, you should discuss this with each merchant you consider entering an affiliate program with. Ensure that you pay attention to all of the elements surrounding payments so you are clear and confident as to when you are going to be paid by the merchant.

## Do I need to pay taxes on my earnings?

Affiliate marketing earnings are considered an income, therefore most states and/or provinces will require you to pay taxes on them. In order to know more about this subject, you should consult your accountant or a tax representative who can help you determine what the taxable rate is and how much you should save to ensure that you are not short come tax season.

## What if I don't like the product?

For some affiliate agreements, you are required to receive and test a product before promoting it. In these types of agreements, it is important that you discuss this element with the merchant. Ensure that you are both clear on what will happen should you determine that you are not a fan of the product you have opted to try. The best thing to do is ensure that you only enter agreements where you are allowed to send the product back or discard it should you not like the product.

In many cases, merchants will allow for a clause in the agreement where you are allowed to return or discard the used product if you do not like it, on the condition that you provide clear details as to why you did not like the product. Some, however, will still want you to promote the product regardless. In this situation, it is entirely up to you what you choose to do. You may still choose to enter the agreement and hope that you like the product while potentially having to promote a product you don't like to your audience, or you could wait for a better agreement to come along. Remember, if you promote an unlikeable product, you may ruin your trustworthiness among your audience and destroy the likelihood of them purchasing your promoted products again in the future.

# Chapter Three:

## How to Get Started with Affiliate Marketing

There are many steps required to begin earning a profit through affiliate marketing. In fact, there are seven steps, to be exact. These steps will help walk you through the process of getting started and earning a profit quickly. In this chapter, we are going to explore a detailed explanation of what each of these seven steps are and how you can get started right away.

### Find your niche

The first and foremost thing to do is to find your niche. Before you get into blogging or starting your YouTube channel, you should first find the niche market where you can establish yourself. This will help you find your target customers. Before you get started with finding your niche, here are some questions to ask:

- What is it that interests me the most?

  Picking a niche that you are most interested in increases your chances for having success. Because

17

you are likely to be passionate about this topic, you are more likely to have a clear idea of what it is all about and why customers would be interested in purchasing various products. You have a clear perspective from the customer angle, and therefore you know what they would and wouldn't like. This means you can pick products that are specifically geared towards the preferences of your audience.

Your audience will be able to determine if your passion is true or not. They tend to prefer to lean toward people who are passionate about what they are talking about because they are more trustworthy. They know that these people are genuinely interested in promoting quality products and that they are not simply trying to make cash.

Furthermore, you are more likely to stay committed to something that you are actively interested in. By ensuring that you pick a topic you enjoy, you are going to have more fun with the process, therefore making the profit even more passive because you were likely to talk about that topic anyway so at least with affiliate marketing you can get paid for it!

- How lucrative is the niche?

Each niche has its own capacities, and you need to know the capacity of the niche you are interested in. Remember, you are in this to make money so you do need to consider your affiliate marketing potential from a business standpoint. You want to pick a niche that you can exploit and make a lot of money off of, not one that is going to run dry after a few posts because there isn't enough profitability in it.

Niches that have more potential tend to be those that are highly popular. However, these are also the niches that tend to have the most amount of active competition. You want to pick one that you are going to be able to remain competitive in to ensure that you are profitable for a long time. If you feel that you have a great competitive edge in a more popular category, choose that one! If not, try choosing one that may be a little less aggressive and easier for you to generate success in.

- How much time do you have to invest?

Affiliate marketing becomes passive once you have generated a following and have earned the trust of your following. For that reason, you need to have a considerable amount of time to invest in the early stages to ensure that you can generate an audience and earn their trust. In general, the more competitive the market is, the more active you have to stay to prevent yourself from becoming irrelevant. If you were to choose the beauty industry, for example, you would need to be actively posting on a daily basis to engage with your audience and encourage them to purchase through your affiliate links. Smaller and less competitive markets may not require as much activity, but you will still need to remain active in order to build your following.

When it comes to building a following on the internet, there seems to be three primary time-commitment levels. The first is one where you need to be posting on a daily basis. You want to engage with your audience and build an audience, but you don't want to be over posting, or you may seem like a spam page and people won't want to follow you. Once you have a fairly large following, you want to start posting a couple of times a day to really drive your engagement up. Then, once you have comfortably built a level of sustainable engagement with a strong following, you can slow down and start posting a little less. For example, you may start posting daily once again, or even every other day. The more successful you get, the pickier you want to be about the posts you are sharing to ensure that they are extremely high quality. While they should always be high quality, they should improve as you go, which means you are likely going to have to take your time in order to get great pictures to keep your followers satisfied. Alongside those pictures, you can post the occasional affiliate link to start earning your profits!

- How long will this niche remain profitable?

In addition to knowing how profitable a niche is, you also need to know how long it is going to be profitable for. Some niches, such as beauty, are evergreen and you can exploit them for as long as you are willing to maintain your audience and keep posting. Others, however, may be trend-based and will dry up after some time. Since you are operating your affiliate marketing as a business, you need to look at this from a business angle. A healthy niche should be one that has no foreseeable end. If there is one, your profit is going to dry up quickly and you are not going to have much success as an affiliate marketer, largely based on the niche you chose.

The best way to assess your niche is to look at it on a 5- to 6-year term. If the niche is expected to remain strong and healthy for at least that amount of time, it is likely that you have chosen a good one. Otherwise, you may want to consider choosing one that will be more sustainable to prevent you from investing a large amount of work into a niche that will not have a long-term payoff.

- Are there any affiliate programs available for this niche?

  Naturally, you need to ensure that there are actually affiliate programs available for the niche you are considering. While there are programs for almost every niche out there, some may not have any. Alternatively, your niche may have affiliate programs, but there may not be enough for it to really become sustainable.

If you find that your niche has a limited selection, you have two options: you can choose a better niche, or you can commit to that one. If you are going to commit, make sure that you are choosing a niche that has some very strong programs that you can maintain over a long period of time. These should be programs that are going to continue to be profitable even after you've been with them for a few years. If you don't see them being that sustainable, it is strongly advised that you choose a different niche.

## Research

The next step of the process is conducting your research. Once you decide on the niche, you have to find the programs and products that best suit your niche. You might have already started with it while deciding on your niche, and now it is time to do a little more research on it.

You have to spend some amount of time going through the programs and what they offer to you. It is crucial for you to ensure that you go through all the terms to make sure that you know what you are getting into. You will be able to generate a decent income only if you spend time researching the products and know it will be worth the effort.

Here are some pointers to bear in mind.

- You have to look at the types of sellers who are using the network, as it will help you understand how successful the affiliation or affiliate program can be.

- You have to look into the network and check the type of programs and payment systems that exist.

- Ideally, you should look for programs that pay you 50 to 60% commission so that you can make the most of the affiliation. If you are using a platform like Clickbank, then it can be a little higher. The basic idea is to find products and programs that are going to help you make the most of the affiliation.

- If you choose a cost per action scheme, then you have to find programs that pay above $1 and ensure that the products are not too restrictive and can be promoted freely.

- For any physical products that you promote, look for at least $40 and above commissions.

- Before choosing any products and services, you have to ask yourself whether it goes with your image and if people will be willing to buy it. Do not endorse anything that goes against your image.

- You have to analyze the sales pitch that you can use to bag the affiliate and what ideas you can use to promote the products.

- It is essential to check the type of support that the program provides. You should have customer care service numbers that you can call in case you have any queries and have quick solutions to problems.

## Site building

Once you recognize your niche market and research your affiliates, you can move to building your site. This step is all about putting your plans into action. If you already have a website of the blog up and running, then you must work on finding your affiliates. But if you don't have one, then here are the steps to adopt.

- First off, you have to decide upon a domain name and pick something that is unique to you. You have to be recognizable so that people know it's your website. Many popular websites give you the chance to register your domain name, such as GoDaddy.Com. Once you decide on the title, check if it is available and buy it so that you don't lose the chance of getting your desired domain name.

- Once done, you have to set up the blog or website. Look for reliable hosts who give you good features to work with. Some good hosts include BlueHost and GoDaddy.com.

- Next, you have to install WordPress so that you have a CMS to work with. You will be given a one-click option that you can use to install it on your site.

- Next, you have to install the theme and make it unique.

- Once done, you have to add the content. It is this content that will help you find your target affiliates.

- NOTE: When building your site, it is now a legal requirement to include a disclaimer that your site may contain affiliate links attached to it. You should have a disclaimer on your website in an easy to find area that informs viewers that your content may include affiliate links, in order to ensure that you do not infringe on any legal requirements with your business.

## Making the Content

The content you post and create is absolutely crucial when it comes to affiliate marketing. This is your "advertising", so you need to take it as seriously as large companies take their own marketing campaigns. The content you create is what will draw people to your site and encourage them to shop your affiliate links, or it will send people away looking for someone more interesting and relatable.

Content is truly the key when it comes to successful marketing. This is the key that will unlock a large audience, attract customers, and earn you profit. The more of an audience you build and the more customers you attract, the larger your affiliate deals will become, meaning that you will be able to earn more profit. It is absolutely imperative that you stay highly focused on the quality of content that you are producing and that it is worthy of earning a healthy and loyal following.

There is a lot to know when it comes to creating content. First, you should know that there are different types of content that people come for. Depending on the niche you are in and the purpose of your site, you will want to pick a content theme that serves your audience. The following list shows an example of some of the most popular and successful themes of content that you can create for your audience.

- Reviews

Building websites around reviews is a great way to start your affiliate marketing company. People love seeing reviews and hearing about other people's experiences with products they are interested in. If you wish to create a niche for yourself where you can stand out and be the one people look to, you need to be reviewing products that have not already been reviewed by a large portion of existing reviewers. In other words, you need to be innovative and stay ahead of the curve. The best way to do this is to constantly search for new affiliate opportunities and to continually pay attention to product trends for your unique niche so that you can stay on top of them and review the products before anyone else.

- Current Affair Blogs

Many people turn to the internet as an opportunity to find information. More and more, people are tuning into the internet to find relevant information. If you give them the information they are looking for, you can instantly catapult your popularity. Because you will become known for your new content, people will continue coming back to your blog to learn about current affairs in your particular niche.

- Free Courses

People tend to look for places where they can have free content. This can be an eBook, dance lessons, singing lessons, language lessons, make up instructions, etc. All these happen to be niche ideas that you can use to find your target audience. You can make use of email marketing to generate leads and get more and more people to view your videos or visit your blog page. A good way of monetizing it is by incorporating the products that you wish to sell so that you can promote them effortlessly. You have to know that nobody will be interested in generic content and need something specific. Generic content leads to lesser traffic and, in turn, lower sales. So you have to put in the effort of giving them value-based products that are sure to keep them coming back for more.

After you have chosen your theme, you need to know how to create quality content for your website or account. The following checklist will help you ensure that each piece of content you create is high quality so that your audience will enjoy it. Check it over before posting any content.

- Catchy title

- Engaging verbal content

- Attractive imagery

- SEO optimized

- Relevant and new content

- Clear and to-the-point

- Properly categorized on your blog

- Relevant and trending tags

## Building an audience

The next task for you is to build a large audience base. The audience is what will help you get your affiliate marketing rolling. Many people assume that an audience will start building as soon as you get your blog rolling. But this is not true, as you have to put in the effort of finding an audience and retaining them. Remember that you will require a steady stream of views to maintain popularity. For this, you have to do certain things that will keep your audience interested in what you are putting out. Here are some tips to help you increase your customer base.

- Use social media

Social media is a wildly popular networking opportunity that virtually everyone is on. With so many different social media platforms available at this time, you can guarantee that your niche's audience exists on social media somewhere. The first key is to find out what platform they use most. Each platform has unique purposes and benefits, as well as a unique audience range. Do some research to ensure that you are most active on the platforms where your niche's audience will be most active. You don't want to market to your audience in a platform where they hardly exist!

Ensure that you link all of your platforms together so that you can share among them and people can find you. Keep your handles (usernames) the same as well, as this will make you identifiable and findable among your audience. They can easily key in the same handle on any platform and find you on there. Then, actively post on each platform so that people know you're engaged on it. Furthermore, take the time to reply to those who take the time to message you or comment on your content. As well, you can go through and like and comment on their stuff, making it clear that you care about them and about increasing their loyalty to you and your content.

- Make use of collaborations

  Collaborating in affiliate marketing means that you work together with other influencers and affiliate marketers to cross-promote to each other's audiences. If there is someone who has a lot more subscribers and/or followers than you do, a great way to collaborate is to ask them to guest post on your blog or do a special video for your page. Alternatively, you may ask if you could create special content for their blog or page.

  Some affiliate marketers who are much larger than you may require you to pay a fee in order to collaborate with them, but in many cases this is completely worthwhile as it can help you reach a much larger audience. Just like they currently have more success in reaching your audience and promoting products than you do, they will likely also have a great deal of success helping you reach your audience and increase your own success. Do as many collaborations as you can with relevant people in your niche to increase the amount of engagement you get and build a larger audience base.

- SEO content

Search engine optimized content, or SEO content, is an important thing to consider when you are building an audience. Creating content that is SEO optimized means that you are far more likely to end up at the top of a search engine results list when your audience is searching for the same products you are promoting. Using relevant hash tags on social media and using proper keywords for your audience are both great ways to use SEO to your advantage. Keeping a blog is also helpful as it helps you organically increase your keyword count and keep your website content updated so search engines are more likely to show you at the top of their lists.

- Email lists

Many business owners and marketing experts agree that email lists are incredibly important when you are building a business. This simple tool helps increase awareness and build engagement with your audience. Keeping a regular email newsletter that you send to your audience is a great way to personally reach them and keep your blog or website name in front of them on a consistent basis.

When you engage in newsletter marketing, ensure that you are sending regular newsletters. Sending one per week or more is a great way to keep your name in front of your audience. You can use websites like MailChimp or Ontraport to create newsletters in advance and schedule their release so that you don't have to create new newsletters each day. Ensure that you use the content checklist to keep your newsletters fresh and attractive to your audience.

- Paid advertisements

Paid advertisements are a great way to increase your reach and access more of your audience. When you use paid advertisements effectively, you increase your ability to be seen and you make it more likely for your audience to find you. Because websites like Facebook, Google, Amazon, and others are being paid to promote you, they are more likely to display you to your audience instead of your competition. Make sure you are using effective and attractive marketing strategies in your paid advertisements to get the best results. The content checklist can help with this process as well.

## Promoting Merchants

This is the most crucial part of the monetization process with affiliate marketing. That is, promoting your merchants. When you enter an agreement with a merchant, you enter on the contingency that you are going to market their products to your audience. It is crucial that you uphold that part of your agreement and market to your audience so that they can find your merchants and make purchases. Not only will this help you uphold your part of the agreement, but it is also necessary if you are going to get paid. After all, if you don't post links for people to purchase from, how will they be able to purchase through your affiliate links at all?

Here are some examples of how you can promote affiliate products through your online presence:

- Review Products

  Product reviews are a great way to promote products while also building content. Share with your audience about how much you loved a particular product and let them know about all of the many reasons why they would likely want to purchase the product as well. Then, ensure that you share your affiliate link at every opportunity you have without looking like you are creating spam.

When you are creating product reviews, be sure that you are always completely honest about the products you have used. If there are pitfalls or particular drawbacks about a given product, be sure to be honest about it. However, do so in a positive light. You never want to badmouth a company that has allowed you to do an affiliate program with them as this may lead to legal issues, as well as decreasing your chances of having future affiliate programs with other merchants. You need to keep everything positive and friendly, yet still honest. Never fabricate a review for greater sales volumes as this can deplete your credibility and prevent people from purchasing anything you recommend in the future.

- Post Ads

Banner ads are a great way to increase sales and promote products. If you have a website or a blog, which you should, use banner ads on your page as an opportunity to increase your promotional opportunities. Banner ads have existed for a very long time and they have continued to be successful in the realm of promotions. The ad should have an attractive image of the product or merchant you are promoting and it should be a button that clicks through to the merchant's website using your unique affiliate link. That way, anytime someone shops through it they are using your affiliate link and you are being paid for it. Some affiliate programs will even pay extra for you to promote in this way, so be sure to pay attention to the agreement and see about this clause.

- Context Links

Context links are links where you turn a certain set of words on your website, typically in a blog post, into a link. For example, when you see (click here) turned into a hyperlink, that would be a context link. Context links can be used on titles, product names, merchant names, or any other suitable spot on your website to help link your audience to your affiliate link. You can use these in addition to regular links as an opportunity to increase the availability of the link and the likelihood that your reader will actually click on it. For example, say you run a food-based blog and you are selling the ingredients used to make the products. You could create context links on each ingredient to each unique product using your affiliate link so that your readers could purchase additional ingredients through that link and you earn some cash in the process.

- Email Promotions

In addition to providing interesting and relevant content, you can also include affiliate promotions in your emails. Linking products, chatting about a particular product in the body of the email and providing a link, and otherwise promoting products through this content is a great way to maximize your reach and create an easy to locate and personally addressed purchasing opportunity for your audience.

- Discounts and Giveaways

Many times people turn to affiliate links for the discounts that are often attached to them. As previously mentioned, in many cases affiliate programs allow for affiliates to provide exclusive discounts to their readers that are accessed by using the affiliate's link or unique discount code. Providing your audience with these exclusive codes is a great way to maximize your reach because everyone loves a good discount! Not only does it encourage people who were on the fence to make the decision to purchase, but it also encourages those who were already interested in purchasing to go through you for that extra bonus. When you are known for sharing not only great products but also great deals, you are far more likely to have return viewers who are looking for a good opportunity.

Another option is giveaways! Many merchants will help you offer an exclusive giveaway to your audience to help increase the marketability of your campaign. Not only does this help you market their product and expand the reach of their audience, but it also does the same for yours. People love free stuff and will be likely to check back frequently if they know that you often host giveaways to get free product into the hands of your audience. Look for programs and opportunities that enable you to provide giveaways so that you can really engage your audience and maximize your reach.

Be sure that when you are organizing discounts and giveaways that you pay close attention to the agreement you have made with the merchant. Some may outline particular rules or guidelines in accordance with said discounts or giveaways, and it is important that you are clear on what these particular guidelines are. You never want to break the terms of an agreement in your business dealings!

## Repeat

The last step of the process is repeating all the above steps. You have to adopt the same measures for all the new businesses that you set up. It is important to keep continuing what you are doing so that your audience base can be consistently expanded and you have more businesses to fall back on.

Here is a review of all the steps

- Picking your niche

- Researching the affiliate programs that will work for your niche

- Building your website, blog or channel

- Creating the content that will pull in your audience

- Promoting affiliate products

- Continuing this process

Once you get the hang of it, you will be able to keep up with the processes and consistently utilize affiliate marketing to keep your stream of passive income going up.

# Chapter Four:

## Types of Affiliate Program Platforms

By now, you should have a clear understanding of what affiliate marketing is and how you can begin making sales right away through your own affiliate marketing business. In this chapter, we are going to take a look at some popular platforms that you can use to help you connect with merchants and start applying for affiliate marketing programs in your unique niche.

## Clickbank

Clickbank is a huge and popular platform to find affiliate links. It is one of the oldest and has been in business for 17 years. It is a platform that focuses on digital information products. There are over 6 million products to choose from and about 200 million customers who already use the website around the world. But you have to be a little careful while choosing the products, as not all will be reliable.

## Rakuten

Rakuten was previously known as Buy.com and has since grown in size and stature. Rakuten is one of the most widely used e-commerce websites in the world. There are more than 90,000 products to pick from and around 40,000 stores to choose from. They have over 19 million customers and several programs and models that can help you kick-start your affiliate journey. Choose products based on their rankings, and you are sure to make the most of your affiliations.

## CJ Affiliate

CJ Affiliate is a platform that can help you reach out to millions of consumers thanks to their vast network base. Several big companies are part of the platform such as Mediaplex and Greystripe. You can use these to pick the right affiliate program.

## Amazon Associates

I'm sure Amazon is the one name that you will instantly recognize as the company does not need any introduction. Amazon.com is well reputed and is the largest retailer in the USA. Amazon affiliates help millions of people tap into their product sales and make the most of it. You can advertise from thousands of products and thousands of stores and make the most of your affiliation with them. Amazon is also one of the highest paying websites, and you can make anywhere from 4% to 20% from sales.

## Avantlink

Avantlink is a leader regarding affiliation networks and happens to have advanced technologies and cutting-edge systems that help in making it a leader. They regularly update and upgrade thereby giving them an edge over others. They assist in implementing tools and technologies that emphasis on quality over quantity. You can make the most of your affiliation opportunity by linking with them and capitalizing on their advanced approach.

## Revenue wire

Revenue wire is a global affiliate network that is popular with a large number of companies that it hosts and is said to be on par with Clickbank. It provides incredible service and allows affiliation to over 120 countries.

## Revi media

Revi media is a lead generating website that helps in finding leads for companies. It is owned by an insurance firm and provides products and services related to housing finances, International exchanges, etc. It is one of the widely used websites to promote leads and offer quality services. They own and operate flexible services and payment methods. It also offers advertising programs and partners to help their merchants and affiliates come together. This makes them extremely popular as people do not have to worry about advertising and can use their services to affiliate and promote finance-based products and services.

## Adcombo

Adcombo is a marketing network that makes use of their technologies and help in customizing advertisements and campaigns to reach their customer base. Their primary motive is to reach out to more and more merchants and provide target based services so that it is easier to bridge the gap between them and affiliates. They offer services in many countries and have been working around the world for many years. This means they have the expertise and can help you find the right products and clients.

## ShareASale

ShareASale is one of the most popular affiliate marketing websites on the Internet and has been running for over 15 years. They are known for their speed and accuracy and their fair and just business conduct. They make sure that the programs are tailor-made for their clients and that both parties make the most out of the affiliation.

## EBay

EBay is one of the most popular websites in the world and has an affiliate network that boasts of thousands of products. However, their affiliate program is not well known, and only a few make use of it. The website offers excellent opportunities for people to make use of their popularity and promote products and services.

## Advantage

Advantage is a popular cloud platform the mainly focuses on online commerce and subscriptions for online service companies. There are over 3500 businesses located all over the world and include the likes of FICO, Spyrix, and clever control.

## Flexoffers.com

Flexoffers.com is a leading affiliate network website that helps in building a successful affiliation with several companies and helps in reaching out to thousands of consumers. There are over 4000 advertisers who span in all aspects and data tools that can be used to make the most of the affiliate programs. Flexoffers.com has been given the rank of number 8 in the 20 best affiliate networks to choose from making it one of the most sought-after and widely accepted affiliate marketing networks. Their rewards or incentives based on performance are quite high and can help you make the most of the affiliations.

## Affibank

Affibank is an affiliate tool that can be used to find affiliates and happen to pay one of the highest commission rates in the business. They pay you 75% of the commission from your sales making it one of the most widely used affiliate websites. They make use of their tracking systems thereby making them efficient and trustworthy.

## VigLink

VigLink is an incredible program that you place on your blog. It scans your content for any mention of a product and then turns that product into an affiliate link. Then, you can post that affiliate link into a context link or otherwise include it in the body of your blog. Anytime a reader comes onto your blog, they can then find that particular product through your link. The great benefit of VigLink is that you do not have to go out of your way to find products. Instead, you create a single account with them and they help you discover products by providing you with a list, rather than you having to go searching. It is extremely easy to use, however, you should note that when using it you still need to submit individual applications to the unique merchants involved so that you can get credited and paid for your sales.

## Skimlinks

Similar to VigLinks, Skimlinks will skim your content and provide you with the links to unique products you may have talked about. The primary point where Skimlinks holds an advantage over VigLinks is that once you apply for a Skimlinks account you are not required to apply for any further merchant programs. Instead, you are automatically approved for all merchants that are using Skimlinks to help promote their products. So, unlike VigLinks, you don't have to apply for a new program each time you post a new link.

## Peerfly

Although they are not quite as large as some of the existing programs, Peerfly is still a big enough program that you can rely on them for some great connections. One great thing about Peerfly, however, is that they guarantee each of their affiliates that they will match or exceed the pay from any other network. This means that when you do get connections through them you are guaranteed to make as much, if not more, as you would through other programs.

# Bonus:

## Have the Right Mindset

Although affiliate marketing is a passive income opportunity, it is still a business. Many people think that because it is online and revolves primarily around people's opinions and link posting, that it does not count as a real business, but this is not true. Affiliate marketing should be viewed as a business, especially if you want to be successful at it. And, as with any business, at least 50% of the success you experience will be directly related to your mindset. If you are determined and focused on generating success, then you have significantly higher chances of generating success in your business. Here are 6 key points that you need to keep in mind when you are building and running your affiliate marketing business:

- **Have a Purpose**: You should always be very clear on why you chose to start this business, even if that purpose was to increase your income. Some people believe that your purpose needs to be deep and elaborate, but this is not true. The only requirement of your purpose is that is unique to you and that it motivates you. Having a purpose will ensure that any time you face difficulties or you are struggling to create the results you desire that you will always come out on the other end, victorious. Any time difficulties arise in front of you, you must always be ready and motivated to overcome them so that you can experience success in your business.

• **Be Rock Solid**: It is important that you remain rock solid when you are in business. Difficulties are going to arise, struggles are going to happen, and sometimes you may be tested on your patience and perseverance. However, if you stay dedicated and continue working, you know you have the opportunity to come out on top. For this reason, you must be rock solid in your business. Like a rock in the ocean being hit by waves, you must refuse to move. Stay unshakeable, stay solid, and stand your position. If you are unwavering, then your success shall be, too.

• **Kaizen**: This is a Japanese word that means continuous improvement, and it's the philosophy that you have to apply to your business. If you want to generate success, you have to constantly be looking for opportunities to improve upon what you have already done. No matter how good you are when you start, there are always opportunities to improve on what you have already created.

Improvement is important in business for two primary reasons: first, if you don't improve you will fall behind. Business is a fluid game and the stakes are constantly changing. There are always new marketing strategies and trends being introduced, and you have to stay on top of them. This is how you stay relevant. Furthermore, you want to do your best to be at the leader of it all. By constantly improving on your own success, you create the opportunity for you to become the trendsetter, rather than remaining as the trend follower. When you are seen as a leader like this, your business will inevitably improve.

- **Process Oriented**: You must always focus your attention on the process and not the outcome. The process of creating your business is where the opportunities for improvement lie. This is also where you get to create value and content for your audience. If you rush too quickly because you want results, you are not going to be creating the materials that you need to actually gain those results. In the end, you will end up on a fruitless mission where you are chasing something that is not available to you, merely because you are not paying attention.

The processes within your business carry a significant amount of importance. When you pay attention to them, you can easily identify where you are succeeding and where you are struggling. This means you can effortlessly discover opportunities to do better in the future, and you can increase on the success you have already created. If you want to be successful, you need to practice mastering every aspect of your business. The entire process should be paid attention to so that you provide such a significant amount of value to your customer that earning profits as a result of your effort is inevitable.

• **Believe**: Remember before seeing something you, have to believe it is possible. Taking the time to regularly revisit your belief in your vision and honing that vision is a great way to increase your belief in your abilities and make your dreams come to life. There is a common story told around the power of belief that goes like this:

> For many years, running a four-minute mile was the world record. People could not seem to break this record, likely because they had been told it was unbeatable. Several people tried but every single one

failed because they believed it was not possible. One day, someone decided he was going to break the four-minute mile. He lead himself to believe it was possible and trained like he had never trained before. After much training, he beat the four-minute mile. People were in awe and completely shocked at his abilities. However, suddenly many runners were beating the four-minute mile. They now believed it was possible, and so it became possible for them.

As you can see, holding the belief of something in your mind and telling yourself that you are capable is an incredibly powerful way to increase your abilities, and your likelihood of becoming successful. So, if you want to be a successful affiliate marketer, you must first genuinely believe that it is a possibility for you and that you are capable of achieving this goal.

- **Quality and Contribution**: The first goal on any activity you set out to fulfill for your business needs to focus on one thing, every time: quality. Every time you create content, post pictures, share products, or otherwise interact with your audience, you must always be confident that you are sharing quality material. The information you are sharing in posts or articles should be valuable and should help your audience in some way. The images you share should be high quality and attractive, while also clearly displaying exactly what you have set out to display. The products you are promoting should always match the high quality standards that you carry for your own business so that your audience continues to trust your judgment and support your business.

If you focus on the customer in all respects and you do your absolute best to continually provide them with high quality and value through everything that you do, it is inevitable that your following will grow. Pay attention to what people are interested in and focus on giving them what they want and need, not on what you think you can do to make a quick sale. Remember, generating long-term loyalty and building your credibility will establish lasting results. Selling out to make quick sales will result in you losing your loyal following and, therefore, your business not working. Make your audience the focus of everything that you do.

If you take your time and implement these six steps in your business, you will already be halfway to creating a powerful and successful business not only online, but also offline. It is crucial that you stay focused, provide value, believe in yourself and your abilities, and stay unwavering in your purpose so that you are always working toward success in your business. Don't let hardships, difficult times or other struggles hold you back from the success you are eager to achieve. Charge forward and the success will be yours!

# <u>Conclusion</u>

I thank you once again for choosing this book and hope you had a great time reading it.

The primary aim of this book was to educate you on the basics of affiliate marketing and how you can use it to increase your monthly income. I hope you have a good time finding your affiliates and earning a passive income.

Finally, if you enjoyed this book, then I'd like to ask you for a favor, would you be kind enough to leave a review for this book on Amazon? It'd be greatly appreciated!


Thank you and good luck!


Robert J. Murphy